50 MATHEMATICAL PUZZLES AND PROBLEMS

GREEN COLLECTION

**From the International Championship of Mathematics
Fédération Française des Jeux Mathématiques**

Gilles Cohen, Editor
Éditions POLE

Key Curriculum Press
Innovators in Mathematics Education

Éditions POLE

Coordinator: Michel Criton
Translator: Jean-Christophe Novelli
Editor: Gilles Cohen
Reading and Editing Committee: Julien Cassaigne, Francis Gutmacher, Jon Millington,
   Bernard Novelli, Jean-Christophe Novelli, Lucien Pianaro
Problem Authors: Gilles Cohen, Michel Criton, Francis Gutmacher, Gilles Hainry,
   Manuel Lucas, Patrice Lucas, Bernard Novelli, Zbigniew Romanowicz, Dominique Souder

Key Curriculum Press

Project Administrator: Heather Dever
Editorial Assistant: Kyle Bridget Loftus
Mathematics and Translation Reviewer: Dudley Brooks
Production Editor: Jennifer Strada
Copy Editor: Margaret Moore
Production Director: Diana Jean Parks
Production Coordinator: Laurel Roth Patton
Compositor: Laurel Roth Patton
Cover Designer: Caroline Ayres
Prepress and Printer: Malloy Lithographing, Inc.

Executive Editor: Casey FitzSimons
Publisher: Steven Rasmussen

Key Curriculum Press, 1150 65th Street, Emeryville, CA 94608, 510-595-7000
editorial@keypress.com
http://www.keypress.com

Éditions POLE, 31 Avenue des Gobelins, 75013 Paris, France

Printed in the United States of America
10 9 8 7 6 5
ISBN 978-1-55953-498-7

❖ PREFACE ❖

The International Championship of Mathematics and Logic has been held in France by the FFJM (Fédération Française des Jeux Mathématiques) for more than ten years. Writers for these championships have generated over a thousand original puzzles, which are regularly gathered and published in French by Éditions POLE. Key Curriculum Press is pleased to be able to offer a selection of these problems, translated into English.

The problems are organized by difficulty in three collections: the *Green Collection* (grades 6 through 12), the *Orange Collection* (grades 9 through 12), and the *Red Collection* (grade 9 through college level). Full solutions are provided in each book.

We hope you will enjoy these problems. We invite you to participate with the 150,000 other contestants in the International Championship of Mathematics and Logic, which is held once a year in France. For more information, please write to:

FFJM, 1 Avenue Foch, 94700 Maison-Alfort, France

As you work these problems, keep in mind the essential goals of the championship: to apply reasoning more than knowledge, and to find not only one but all of the solutions to a problem.

Éditions POLE
Key Curriculum Press

❖ CONTENTS ❖

Chapter 4 ❖ Divide and Conquer

Chapter 5 ❖ Calculation

Chapter 6 ❖ Using Logic

CHAPTER 1

Using Symmetry

1❖The Paper Staple

I fold a sheet of paper four times, each fold being perpendicular to the previous one.

Then I staple the thick rectangular folded sheet. On second thought, I remove the staple and unfold the paper. These folds have created 16 rectangles, *A, B, C, D, E, F, G,* and *H,* as shown below. Each rectangle has a staple mark.

A	B	C	D
E	F	G	H
I	J	K	L
M	N	O	P

❖ Given the staple mark on rectangle *M,* find where it is on rectangle *H.*

2 ❖ The Small Notebook

A sheet of paper is divided into eight rectangles, namely, *A, B, C, D, E, F, G,* and *H,* as shown in Figure 1. Rectangle *H* is stapled to the table.

Without unstapling rectangle *H,* you fold the sheet of paper three times, as shown in Figures 1, 2, and 3. You then obtain, by cutting some of the folds, the small notebook shown in Figure 4, on which page 1 is shown.

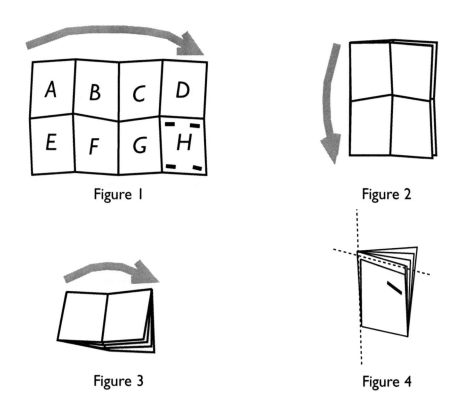

Figure 1

Figure 2

Figure 3

Figure 4

❖ If you number the pages from 1 to 16, what is the letter of the rectangle corresponding to page 9?

3 ❖ Patty Cake's Tart

Patty Cake cooks a tart that has the following unique shape. This tart is intended for four people.

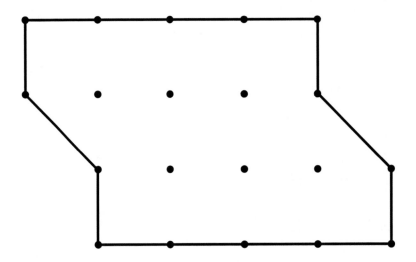

❖ Cut Patty's tart into four parts of exactly the same size and shape.

4 ❖ The Small Enclosure

To build an enclosure on this grid, you have to put black squares on the grid so that they enclose other white squares.

Using four squares, it's possible to enclose one white square (shown on the left).

Using six squares, it's possible to enclose two white squares (shown on the right).

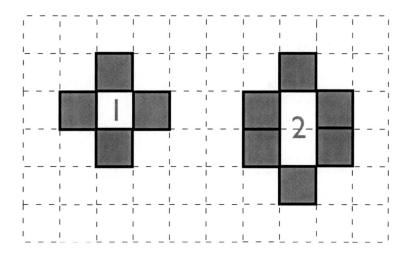

❖ What is the maximum number of white squares that can be enclosed using nine black squares?

5 ❖ The Path of the Sunflower

Professor Sunflower has invented a new species of sunflower. The stem of this sunflower is 62 centimeters long, and it forms a quarter circle. The flower follows the path of the sun, completing a circle in 24 hours.

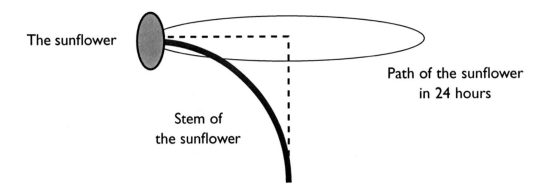

The sunflower

Stem of
the sunflower

Path of the sunflower
in 24 hours

❖ What is the distance the sunflower covers in 24 hours?

6 ❖ Washington Square

Farmer George has a square meadow. He wants to split it into four lots of the same shape, each containing one of the existing pear trees (marked P on the map) and one of the existing cherry trees (marked C on the map).

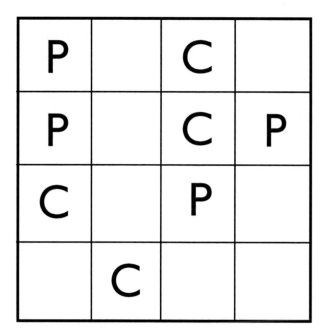

❖ Help George divide his meadow.

7 ❖ The Cedars of Lebanon

Mr. Woodhouse's property, which can be represented by a 5 × 5 square, contains five marvelous cedars of Lebanon. Mr. Woodhouse has four daughters and wants to divide his property according to the following conditions:

- The property is to be divided into five lots of equal area.
- Each daughter will have a cedar on her lot.
- The daughters' lots will all have the same shape (reflected or rotated).
- Mr. Woodhouse has a differently shaped lot, also with a cedar, which is all one piece.
- Mr. Woodhouse's lot is connected by a side to each of his daughters' lots.
- Each daughter's lot is connected by a side to exactly two of her sisters' lots.

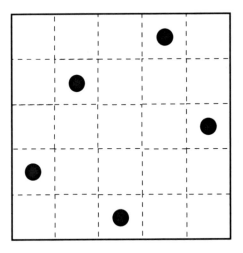

❖ Help Mr. Woodhouse divide his property.

8 ❖ The Six Oaks

Mr. Hawk wants to divide his rectangular property (see the map) between his two sons according to these conditions:

- The house belongs to both sons.
- Both parts of the property have the same shape.
- Each part is connected (that is, in one piece) and has three oaks, which must not lie in a straight line. (The oaks are represented by dots on the map.)

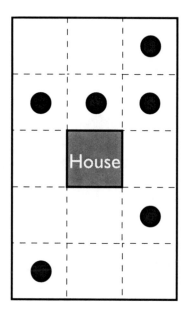

❖ Following the lines of the squares, find a solution to this problem.

9 ❖ Albert's Map

Albert has colored the map of an imaginary continent. In the center of this continent is a lake surrounded by 14 countries, as shown below.

The numbers from 1 to 4 represent four different colors that Albert has used to color the map. Adjacent countries have two different colors.

Albert used:

- color 1 three times,
- color 2 three times,
- color 3 four times, and
- color 4 four times.

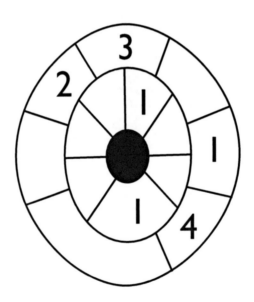

❖ Give a possible coloring of Albert's map.

CHAPTER 2

Using Numbers

10 ❖ Catastrophe at Beatrice's

A terrible hailstorm has devastated the hive! Beatrice has been appointed to rebuild the damaged cells.

Looking at the enormous hole, Beatrice would like to know how many faces of the hive (a face is the side of a hexagon) have been damaged or destroyed.

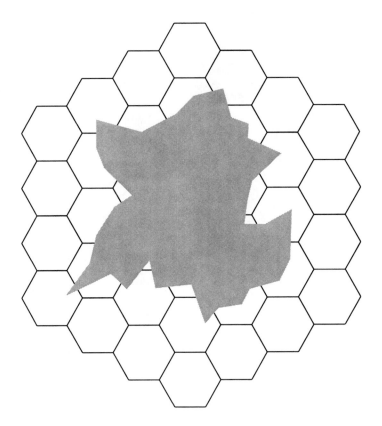

❖ How many faces will Beatrice have to repair or rebuild?

11 ❖ A Cut a Day

On Sunday my tailor received 16 meters of cloth. On the next day, Monday, he cut off 2 meters. On the following days, he cut off 2 meters of material every day, except on the following Sunday, when he rested.

❖ On which working day did the tailor make his last cut?

12 ❖ The Training of Tim Speed

Tim Speed, the bicycle champion, trains every day. Every morning he starts from the small town of Pedalton, where he lives, and reaches the one-way main road using one of the seven minor roads shown on the map. He then travels on part of the (one-way) road and gets back home by another minor road.

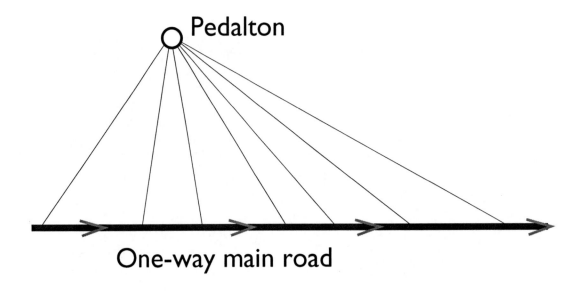

❖ How many different routes can Tim take?

13 ❖ Letters and Numbers

Forty-five has an interesting property: The sum of its digits (4 + 5 = 9) is equal to its number of letters (not counting the hyphen).

❖ How many numbers from 1 to 69, including 45, have a number of letters equal to the sum of their digits? What are these numbers?

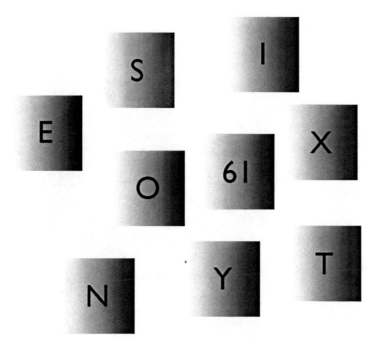

14 ❖ Tom's Book

Tom is looking at his encyclopedia of mathematical games. It has four unnumbered cover pages and 256 interior pages, numbered from 1 to 256. The left pages have even numbers, the right pages have odd numbers.

Tom opens his encyclopedia at random. He adds up the six digits of the two page numbers in front of him. This sum is the greatest it can be.

❖ What is the number on the left page?

15 ❖ One Hundred, Nine Tens, Six Ones

The teacher has just shown, by putting objects in the hundreds, tens, and units columns, that 196 can be represented with 16 objects (see the diagram below).

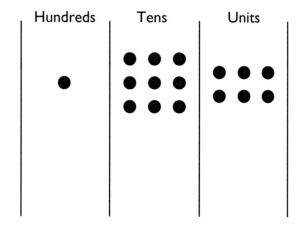

Matthew exclaims, "If we can put more than 10 objects in each column, we can represent 196 with many more objects!"

"That's right. Our method is the best one, because we use the least possible number of objects," replies the teacher. "With your method, would you be able to represent 196 with exactly 70 objects?"

A moment later, Matthew and Matilda both found solutions representing 196 with exactly 70 objects, but their solutions were different.

❖ Give both Matthew's and Matilda's solutions.

16 ❖ Six in a Rectangle

Fill the five blank circles shown in the diagram with the numbers from 2 to 6 so that the difference between any two numbers connected by a line is always greater than 1.

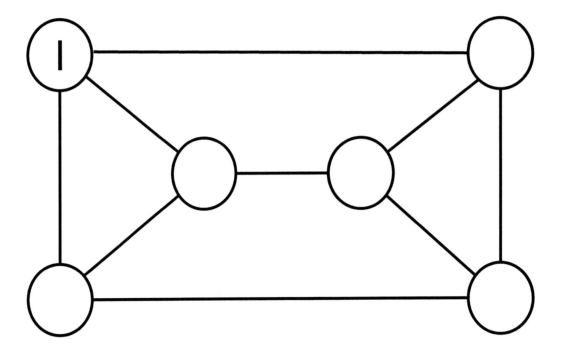

50 Mathematical Puzzles and Problems ◆ *Green Collection*
©2001 Key Curriculum Press

❖ CHAPTER 3 ❖

More and Less

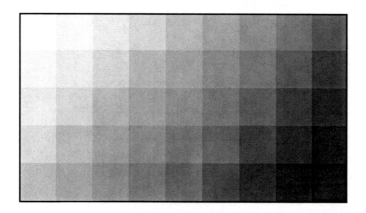

17 ❖ The Bottle

Today is Vanessa's birthday. At the beginning of her party, the bottle of pineapple juice was full and it weighed 1.225 kilograms.

In the middle of the party, the bottle was half empty and it weighed 784 grams.

When everyone left, the bottle was empty.

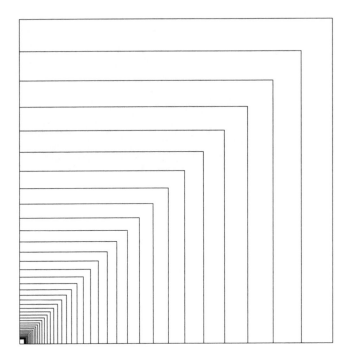

❖ What did the empty bottle weigh?

18❖Lolly's Lollipop

Lolly leaves her school in Paris and runs down the street to Mme. Bonbon's shop, which sells candies. She buys a lollipop for 15 centimes and hands Mme. Bonbon 1 franc, which is equal to 100 centimes.

"I'm sorry, Lolly, I can't give you any change," says Mme. Bonbon.

So Lolly hands her 50 centimes instead.

"I'm very sorry, I still can't give you any change. I have in my cash register an amount between 50 centimes and 1 franc in gold coins. If you had a 20-centime coin, I could give you change."

❖ How much money is in Mme. Bonbon's cash register?

Note: In France, the gold coins can have a value of 5, 10, or 20 centimes.

19 ❖ A Bag of Candy

Matilda and Matthew share a bag of candies using the following process: Matthew takes a candy; Matilda takes two candies; then Matthew takes three, Matilda takes four, and so on, each taking one candy more than the other had taken.

Matilda is the last one to take the appropriate number of candies, and the bag is then empty.

She then has 10 candies more than Matthew.

❖ How many candies were in the bag?

20 ❖ Skiing

Bernard is skiing down a steep slope of numbers. Each time he goes through a square, he earns the number of points written in that square. While going down, he has the choice between the two squares below the one he's on.

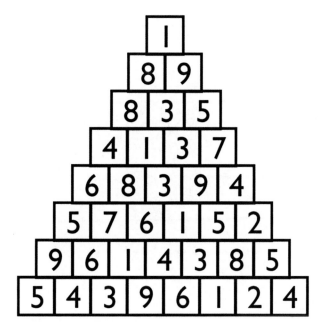

❖ Find the greatest total score Bernard can get.

21 ✦ Enchanted Square

Fill in the nine cells of this 3 × 3 square with the numbers from 1 to 9 so that the sum of the numbers belonging to any given 2 × 2 square (like the gray square) is always the same.

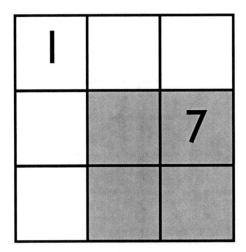

22❖Melancholy

Albrecht Dürer, the great engraver, proved his arithmetical knowledge in the famous engraving *Melancolia*.

In a corner of the engraving there is a magic 4 × 4 square containing in its last row the date of its creation, 1514.

You can easily verify that the sum of four numbers in any horizontal, vertical, or diagonal row, or the four corner squares, or any of the four corner 2 × 2 squares, or the central 2 × 2 square, is always the same.

16	3	2	13
5	10	11	8
9	6	7	12
4	15	14	1

❖ Use the numbers from 1 to 16 to fill in this different magic square, which has the same magic sum as Dürer's: 1514.

16		1	13
9			
			7
	15	14	

---

23 ❖ The Incomplete Table

Here's an addition table to be filled in (for example, $A + H = 15$), given that the sum of the numbers in the bold lined square equals 200 and none of the numbers are the same.

+	E	7	G	H
A	7			15
3			11	
C				
6				16

❖ Find the numbers that belong in row C.

50 Mathematical Puzzles and Problems ◆ *Green Collection*
©2001 Key Curriculum Press

24 ❖ Lady Adelaide Adler

Is it because she's old, because she's left-handed, or just because the British drive on the left? At any rate, Lady Adelaide Adler stubbornly does addition from left to right.

So instead of writing

$$
\begin{array}{r}
7\,5 \\
+\,8\,6 \\
\hline
1\,6\,1
\end{array}
$$

she writes

$$
\begin{array}{r}
7\,5 \\
8\,6\,+ \\
\hline
5\,2\,1
\end{array}
$$

She first adds the numbers in the left column and then proceeds to the right column, and also writes down the digits of the "result" from left to right.

Astonishingly, today Lady Adelaide's method has given the right answer. Here is part of her addition, written in her own peculiar way:

$$
\begin{array}{r}
4\,. \\
.\,.\,+ \\
\hline
1\,2\,1
\end{array}
$$

❖ What is the number in the second row?

25 ❖ The Five Weights

You are given five different weights, marked 1 lb, 2 lb, 5 lb, 6 lb, and 10 lb.

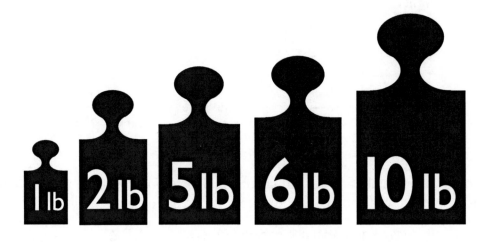

❖ How many different weights can you obtain using these weights?

CHAPTER 4

Divide and Conquer

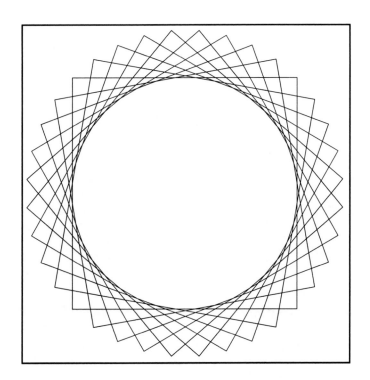

26 ❖ Mary's Flowers

Mary lives in the middle of a large garden. One day, she decides to cut as many flowers as her age in years. Then, each day, she cuts twice as many flowers as the day before. On the fifth day, following the same rule, she prepares a huge bouquet that has as many flowers as her grandma's age in years. Mary's grandma is 60 years older than Mary.

❖ How many flowers has Mary cut altogether?

27 ⋄ The Eye of the Cyclops

Kevin is afraid of making a mistake in math class, so he always carries a multiplication table with him:

×	2	3	4	5	6	7	8	9
2	4	6	8	10	12	14	16	18
3	6	9	12	15	18	21	24	27
4	8	12	16	20	24	28	32	36
5	10	15	20	25	30	35	40	45
6	12	18	24	30	36	42	48	54
7	14	21	28	35	42	49	56	63
8	16	24	32	40	48	56	64	72
9	18	27	36	45	54	63	72	81

His older brother Matthew has made him a square mask with a hole in the center. The mask covers exactly nine squares of the multiplication table, and through the hole you can see the center number.

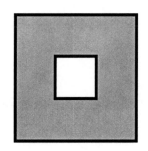

Today, Matthew told Kevin that the sum of the eight hidden numbers is 288.

❖ What is the center number?

28 ❖ Marathon

Six runners wearing numbers from 1 to 6 took part in a race. The runners wearing even numbers finished in odd-numbered places. The runners wearing multiples of 3 finished in places that are not multiples of 3. Lastly, the runners wearing numbers greater than 3 took the first three places.

❖ What was the order of the runners on the finish line?

29 ❖ Numerical Maze

Theseus enters a large maze at the square numbered 95. He can exit only from the square numbered 96.

He can go from his square to an adjacent one only if the two numbers have a common divisor greater than 1 (that is, both numbers are divisible by the same number, which is greater than 1), and he cannot use the same square twice.

Entrance →

95	105	11	14	18	49
28	65	26	99	45	
36	117	119	34	85	
121	133	91	92	46	
64	57	111	296	69	96

Exit →

❖ Show Theseus a way out of the maze.

30 ❖ Granddad's Age

Granddad Joss was born in the 20th century. The sum of the digits of his birth year is divisible by 4. Grandma Teresa was born 1 year after her husband, Joss, but the sum of the digits of her birth year is also divisible by 4. In 2001, the sum of their ages was more than 100 years.

❖ What is Granddad Joss's birth year?

31 ❖ The Smallest of the Great

Giles's numbers are the multiples of 1, 2, 3, 4, 5, 6, 7, 8, 9, and 10.

❖ What is the smallest of Giles's numbers?

32 ❖ The Holey Alphabet

The printer at FFJM (Fédération Française des Jeux Mathématiques) has a defect: All of the "holey" letters of the alphabet (a, b, d, e, and so on), when printed, have their holes completely inked in. Each ink refill is expected to print exactly one million letters. All of the letters printed in the usual way use the normal amount of ink, and all of the letters having a hole use exactly three times the normal amount.

a b c d e f g h i j k l m n o p q r s t u v w x y z

A new refill has been put into the printer to print this phrase until the refill is empty:

quarter finals of the tenth mathematical and logical championship

❖ What will the last printed letter be?

33 ❖ The Mathematical Cook

Julius is an apprentice cook. He has to cut cucumbers and put the slices on five plates: *A, B, C, D,* and *E.* There are many slices, so he decides to proceed this way:

Beginning with plate *A,* he puts a slice on *A,* then a slice on *B,* then one on *C,* then one on *D,* then the fifth slice on *E.* Then he starts from *E,* puts a slice on *E,* then a slice on *A,* and so on, and puts the tenth slice on *D.* Then he starts from *D,* puts a slice on *D,* and so on.

He follows this process until the 1,995th slice.

❖ Where does Julius put this final slice?

34 ❖ Spring Forward, Fall Back

Starting from A, that is, a vowel, Juliet moves four letters clockwise and gets to E, which is also a vowel. She proceeds like this:

- If the letter she's on is a vowel, she moves four letters clockwise.
- If the letter is a consonant, she moves three letters counterclockwise.

❖ If we call A her first letter and proceed according to the rule just explained, what will Juliet's 96th letter be?

35 ❖ Zuzu's Petals

Zuzu has just picked a mathflower. She plucks off one petal at a time, saying:

"I love math a little (first petal),
I love math a lot (second petal),
I love math passionately (third petal),
I am madly in love with math (fourth petal),
I don't much like math (fifth petal),
I love math a little (sixth petal) . . ."

The mathflower is an extraordinary flower: It has 95 petals, and when you remove 5 petals, a new petal grows.

❖ When Zuzu plucks off the last petal of the unfortunate flower, how many petals has she plucked and what does she say?

36 ❖ Quotient = rosiviD

If you divide 100,000 by a certain three-digit number, all of whose digits are different, you get a quotient and a remainder. The quotient is equal to the divisor read from right to left.

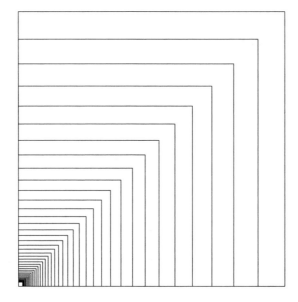

❖ What is this divisor?

CHAPTER 5

Calculation

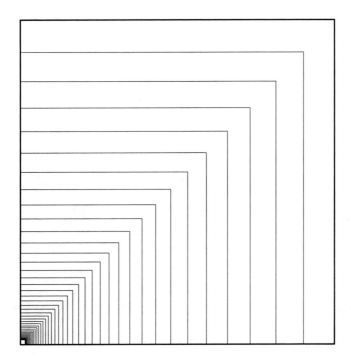

37 ❖ Phone

When the phone rings at home, I never let it ring fewer than three times or more than four. Today my little sister, who likes to count everything, told me that the phone rang 17 times and that I answered all the calls.

❖ How many times did I answer the phone?

38 ❖ Lots of Minuses

If you insert parentheses into the expression $1 - 2 - 3$, you can get two different results: -4 or 2, depending on where you put the parentheses:

$$(1 - 2) - 3 = -1 - 3 = -4 \ or \ 1 - (2 - 3) = 1 + 1 = 2$$

❖ If you insert as many parentheses as you like into the expression
$1 - 2 - 3 - 4 - 5 - 6$, how many different results can you get?

Note: Parentheses can be "nested"—that is, you can have parentheses within parentheses, such as $1 - (2 - (3 - (4 - 5)) - 6$—but you *cannot* have parentheses *directly in front of* minus signs, indicating multiplication, such as $1 - 2 - 3(- 4 - 5 (- 6))$.

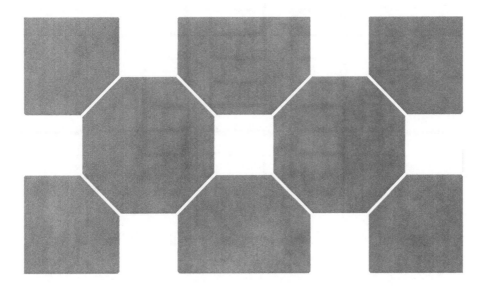

39 ❖ Jacob's Ladder

Jacob has a sliding double ladder. Each of the two parts of the ladder is 2.20 meters long and has 10 equally spaced rungs 20 centimeters apart.

The upper part of the double ladder has two hooks on its lowest rung (see the diagram) that rest on a rung of the lower part of the ladder. But for security reasons, these hooks cannot rest on the topmost rung (AB) of the lower part or on the one below it (CD).

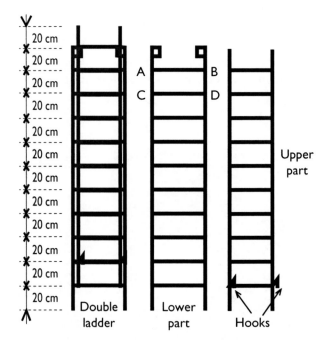

❖ What is the greatest possible length of the ladder within the limits of the security rules?

40 ❖ The Eraser

In the list of numbers above, erase two numbers with a sum of 12 and a difference of 2. Then erase two numbers with a sum of 12 and a product of 32. Next, erase two numbers with a difference of 7 and a product of 78. At the end, erase two numbers such that, when dividing the first by the second, the quotient is 3 and the remainder is 2.

❖ What is the remaining number?

41❖Menhir's Obelisks

Menhir has sculpted a gigantic obelisk of 8 metric tons (1 metric ton = 1,000 kilograms) for Singix's birthday. Today, he is carving a smaller obelisk for the birthday of Singix's dog, Droopix. The dimensions of this obelisk are all a quarter of those of the gigantic obelisk.

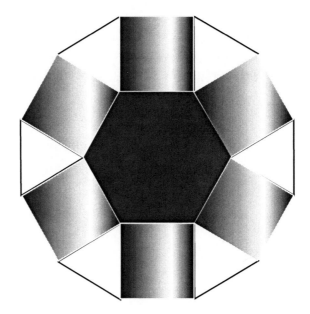

❖ What is the weight of this second obelisk in kilograms?

42 ✦ Of Mice and Sacks

Farmer John has many sacks of wheat and 8 gluttonous cats to protect them. In his granary, there is a crowd of voracious mice: Every night each mouse eats a quarter of a sack of wheat. But the mice are smart and always eat a whole sack before beginning another one. Fortunately for John, every morning each cat eats one mouse.

Last night there were 40 mice in the granary.

❖ When all the mice have been eaten, how many sacks of wheat will have been eaten?

Note: You can assume that the mice always eat as much as they can—John has a lot of wheat.

43 ❖ The Umbrellas of Colorbourg

On Colorbourg Beach, the lifeguard can see 15 red umbrellas and even more green and yellow ones. He also notices that the difference between the number of red and yellow umbrellas is equal to the difference between the number of green and yellow umbrellas.

There are exactly 69 umbrellas on the beach.

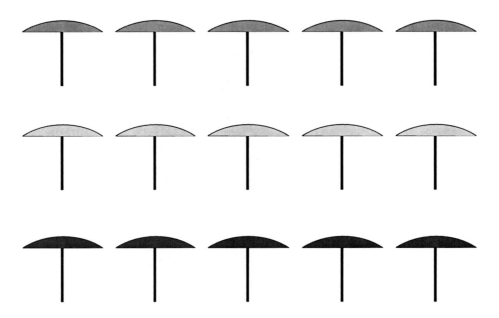

❖ How many green umbrellas are on the beach?

44 ❖ The Two-Key Pocket Calculator

This calculator has only two keys: + 5 and × 5. When you switch it on, it shows 1, and when you press a key the calculator automatically displays the result of the corresponding operation.

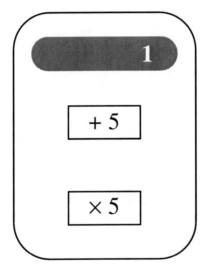

❖ What is the least number of times you must press the keys to get a total of 100?

45 ❖ Thomas's Threes

Thomas, who has forgotten almost everything he learned in school, remembers only the number 3. He doesn't remember the place system, though, so he doesn't know what "33" means. Fortunately, he does remember the + sign, the × sign, and parentheses.

So, for example, to get 63 he uses $(3 + 3 + 3) \times (3 + 3) + 3 \times 3 = 63$.

❖ What is the minimum number of 3's Thomas can write to get 96?

CHAPTER 6

Using Logic

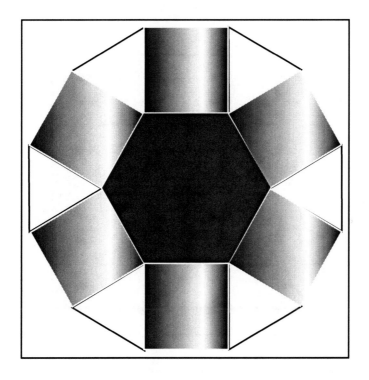

46 ❖ The Maze

I go blindfolded into the maze shown below. As soon as I enter the first room (named M), I follow the wall to the left until I find a new door. I go through this door and then follow the wall to the right until I find a new door. I go through this door and then follow the wall to the left until I find a new door, and so on.

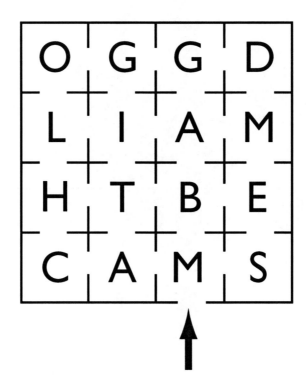

❖ Write down the message formed by the letters corresponding to my blindfolded walk.

50 Mathematical Puzzles and Problems ◆ *Green Collection*
©2001 Key Curriculum Press

47 ❖ Zigzag

I start from the crossroads *A* in the direction indicated by the arrow. At the first crossroads I meet, I take the first road to the left. At the second crossroads I meet, I take the first road to the right. At the next crossroads, I take the first road to the left, and so on.

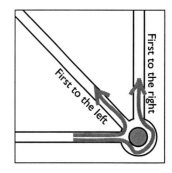

❖ When I'm back at *A*, how many steps have I taken?

Note: Each road between two crossroads is a step. Answer 0 if you think I will never get back to *A*.

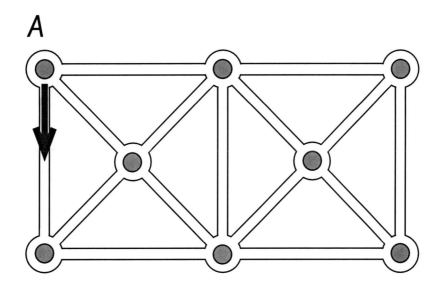

48 ❖ Marion's String

Marion is a well-known maze expert, like her famous grandmother, Ariadne. She enters this maze at *A* with a large ball of string and systematically explores it, getting out at *B*.

Marion has to observe these rules:

- She has to travel along all the corridors.
- Unwinding her ball of string, she can use the same crossroads several times, but the string cannot cross over itself.

❖ Make a clear drawing of a possible route for Marion.

49 ❖ The Shortest Word

Little Ababa plays with the letters of his name. He has invented these rules:

- If he finds an A immediately followed by a B, he can replace them by the sequence BAA.
- If he finds two adjacent B's, he can remove them.
- If he finds three adjacent A's, he can remove them.

❖ If Ababa begins with the word ABABABAABAAB, what is the shortest word he can get?

50 ❖ The Mathematician's Snare

Sarah, Naomi, Alice, Rachel, and Elizabeth are five daughters in a mathematical family. Each of them makes a statement:

1. Sarah: "Paris is spelled with three consonants and two vowels."
2. Naomi: "Mount Snowdon in Wales is 1,085 meters high."
3. Alice: "2 + 3 + 5 + 7 + 11 + 13 + 17 + 19 + 23 = 100."
4. Rachel: "Naomi is a liar."
5. Elizabeth: "Only one of the previous sentences is true."

❖ How many of the statements are true?

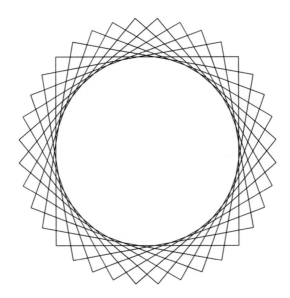

51 ❖ Dominick's Dominoes

Dominick's granddad traveled all over the world when he was younger. Once, he brought back a very special domino set for Dominick. This set has dots from 0 to 9! Unfortunately, Dominick has lost many dominoes, and only the 15 dominoes shown here remain, in a rectangular box.

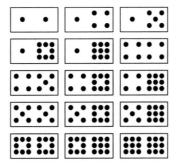

❖ Given the position of the 4-1 domino in the box below, find the position of all the other dominoes (draw a frame around each one).

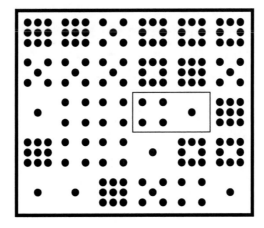

52 ✦ Awale

Every African student knows about the game called "kissoro," "wari," "solo," or even "awale." In this game, you move the tokens (generally grains or small stones) from one cell into the others following rules that differ from one country to another. This problem is derived from these games.

You begin with 24 tokens, placed as shown in the diagram, with 1, 9, 9, and 5 tokens in the cells.

Each move consists of taking one token from each non-empty cell and putting that token in an empty cell. For example, if you choose the empty cell to the right, you get this situation, in which the cells contain 8, 8, 4, and 4 tokens:

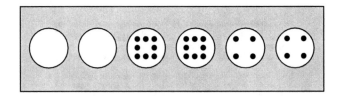

Assuming that there are enough empty cells, you go on and on to the 1,995th position (counting the opening position as the first).

❖ What is the number of tokens in each non-empty cell?

(From the Nigerian Mathematical Games Championship)

❖ SOLUTIONS ❖

1. The Paper Staple

The result is independent of the way the paper has been folded: Two adjacent rectangles are always symmetrical in relation to their common side, and so are their staple marks.

Using symmetries, you can easily find that the staple mark was in the following position in rectangle *H:*

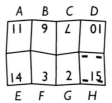

2. The Small Notebook

Imagine doing the reverse operation: You first number the 16 pages, then unfold the paper. You obtain the diagram at far right:

Each number of a rectangle on the nonvisible side is consecutive to the number on the visible side. So 1 is on the same rectangle as 2, 4 as 3, 5 as 6, 8 as 7, 9 as 10, 12 as 11, 13 as 14, and 16 as 15.

So page 9 is on **rectangle D.**

3. Patty Cake's Tart

The diagrams on the following page represent the **13 possible ways** of cutting Patty's tart into four parts of the same size and shape.

Notice that all of these diagrams are symmetrical in relation to the central point of the tart: First, you cut the tart into two symmetrical parts, and since these parts also have a symmetrical shape, you cut each part into two symmetrical parts.

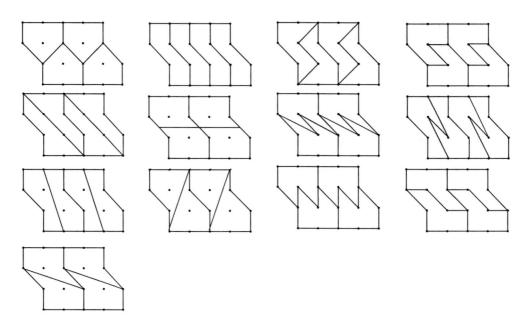

4. The Small Enclosure

The figure shows that nine black squares can enclose
six squares, which is the maximum solution.

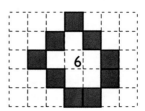

5. The Path of the Sunflower

First, notice that the radius R of the stem of a sunflower
and the radius of the path of its extremity are equal.

So the distance a sunflower covers is equal to the
circumference of the circle of radius R. This length is
equal to four times the length of a quarter circle, 62 cm.

So the distance the sunflower covers in 24 hours is **248 cm.**

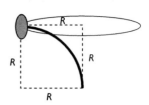

6. Washington Square

Since George wants each part of his square to have its own
pear tree and its own cherry tree, two pear trees or two cherry
trees cannot belong to the same part.

P		C	
P		C	P
C		P	
	C		

Each part may contain four squares. Moreover, the part containing the left uppermost square can have only four different shapes:

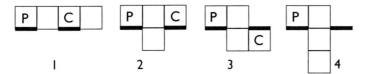

The fourth shape cannot be correct since it does not contain a cherry tree. The third shape used four times cannot fit in the square. The first shape does not respect the rule that each part has one pear tree. So just the second shape remains, and you can verify that it gives the **only solution,** shown here:

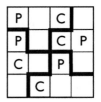

7. The Cedars of Lebanon

Without taking the cedars into account, there are 16 different ways of cutting which satisfy the condition that Mr. Woodhouse's lot is connected to his daughters' lots and the conditions on how the parts touch.

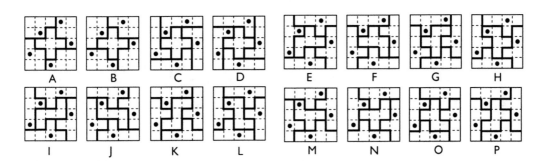

Among these solutions, only F, H, L, and M respect the condition about the cedars. Since the cedars are symmetrical in relation to a diagonal of the square, each solution has a reflection.

The **four solutions** shown here are in fact two distinct solutions and their reflections:

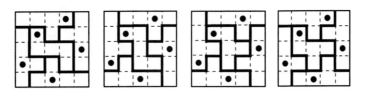

8. The Six Oaks

There are ten possible ways to cut this property into two identical parts:

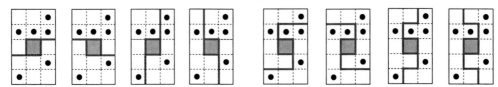

Among all of these, **only the last one** satisfies the condition concerning the oaks.

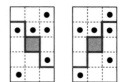

9. Albert's Map

Country *a* must be in color 4 since it is adjacent to three countries colored with the other colors. Country *b* is in color 1 or color 3. Since color 1 has already been used three times, *b* is in color 3. So, *f* is in color 4, *c* is in color 2, and *g* is in color 3. There remain three countries to color, namely, *d, e,* and *h,* and three colors to use, namely, colors 2, 3, and 4.

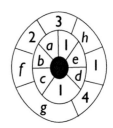

Country *h* is in color 2 or 4. If *h* is in color 2, *e* is in color 4 and *d* is in color 3. If *h* is in color 4, *e* and *d* are in color 2 or 3, leading to two different solutions. This coloring problem has **three solutions,** shown here.

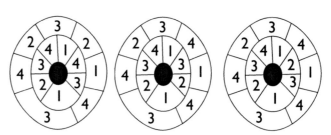

10. Catastrophe at Beatrice's

The diagram shows that Beatrice has to repair or rebuild **43 faces.**

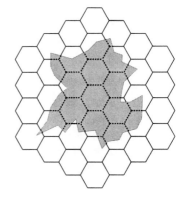

11. A Cut a Day

The diagram below shows that the tailor needs only seven cuts to get eight parts of 2 m each. He will make his cuts on Monday (first cut), Tuesday (second cut), Wednesday (third cut), Thursday (fourth cut), Friday (fifth cut), Saturday (sixth cut), and **Monday** (seventh cut), since he doesn't work on Sunday.

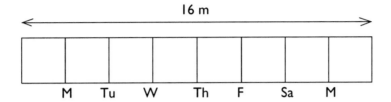

12. The Training of Tim Speed

Let's number the seven minor roads going from Pedalton to the one-way main road as shown below. If Tim takes road 1, he can get back to Pedalton with any road from 2 to 7.

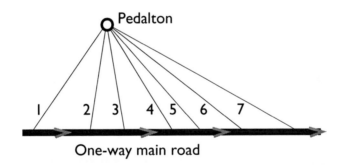

In the same way, if he takes road 2, he can get back to Pedalton with any road from 3 to 7; if he takes road 3, he can get back to Pedalton with any road from 4 to 7; and so on. And if he takes road 6, he can get back only by road 7.

The total number of routes he has at his disposal is

$$6 + 5 + 4 + 3 + 2 + 1 = (6 \times 7)/2 = 21$$

So Tim can use **21 different routes.**

13. Letters and Numbers

With the help of the table below, you can see that **eight numbers** between 1 and 69 have a number of letters equal to the sum of their digits: **four, sixteen, thirty-six, thirty-eight, forty-five, fifty, fifty-four, and sixty-two.**

Number	Written	No. of letters	Sum of the digits	Number	Written	No. of letters	Sum of the digits
1	one	3	1	35	thirty-five	10	3 + 5 = 8
2	two	3	2	**36**	**thirty-six**	**9**	**3 + 6 = 9**
3	three	5	3	37	thirty-seven	11	3 + 7 = 10
4	**four**	**4**	**4**	**38**	**thirty-eight**	**11**	**3 + 8 = 11**
5	five	4	5	39	thirty-nine	10	3 + 9 = 12
6	six	3	6	40	forty	5	4 + 0 = 4
7	seven	5	7	41	forty-one	8	4 + 1 = 5
8	eight	5	8	42	forty-two	8	4 + 2 = 6
9	nine	4	9	43	forty-three	10	4 + 3 = 7
10	ten	3	1 + 0 = 1	44	forty-four	9	4 + 4 = 8
11	eleven	6	1 + 1 = 2	**45**	**forty-five**	**9**	**4 + 5 = 9**
12	twelve	6	1 + 2 = 3	46	forty-six	8	4 + 6 = 10
13	thirteen	8	1 + 3 = 4	47	forty-seven	10	4 + 7 = 11
14	fourteen	8	1 + 4 = 5	48	forty-eight	10	4 + 8 = 12
15	fifteen	7	1 + 5 = 6	49	forty-nine	9	4 + 9 = 13
16	**sixteen**	**7**	**1 + 6 = 7**	**50**	**fifty**	**5**	**5 + 0 = 5**
17	seventeen	9	1 + 7 = 8	51	fifty-one	8	5 + 1 = 6
18	eighteen	8	1 + 8 = 9	52	fifty-two	8	5 + 2 = 7
19	nineteen	8	1 + 9 = 10	53	fifty-three	10	5 + 3 = 8
20	twenty	6	2 + 0 = 2	**54**	**fifty-four**	**9**	**5 + 4 = 9**
21	twenty-one	9	2 + 1 = 3	55	fifty-five	9	5 + 5 = 10
22	twenty-two	9	2 + 2 = 4	56	fifty-six	8	5 + 6 = 11
23	twenty-three	11	2 + 3 = 5	57	fifty-seven	10	5 + 7 = 12
24	twenty-four	10	2 + 4 = 6	58	fifty-eight	10	5 + 8 = 13
25	twenty-five	10	2 + 5 = 7	59	fifty-nine	9	5 + 9 = 14
26	twenty-six	9	2 + 6 = 8	60	sixty	5	6 + 0 = 6
27	twenty-seven	11	2 + 7 = 9	61	sixty-one	8	6 + 1 = 7
28	twenty-eight	11	2 + 8 = 10	**62**	**sixty-two**	**8**	**6 + 2 = 8**
29	twenty-nine	10	2 + 9 = 11	63	sixty-three	10	6 + 3 = 9
30	thirty	6	3 + 0 = 3	64	sixty-four	9	6 + 4 = 10
31	thirty-one	9	3 + 1 = 4	65	sixty-five	9	6 + 5 = 11
32	thirty-two	9	3 + 2 = 5	66	sixty-six	8	6 + 6 = 12
33	thirty-three	11	3 + 3 = 6	67	sixty-seven	10	6 + 7 = 13
34	thirty-four	10	3 + 4 = 7	68	sixty-eight	10	6 + 8 = 14
				69	sixty-nine	9	6 + 9 = 15

14. Tom's Book

Since Tom adds the six digits in front of him, he adds the digits of two consecutive three-digit numbers. Since there are 256 pages, the hundreds digit is 1 or 2.

If the hundreds digit is 1, the numbers that maximize the sum must be 198 and 199, which give the result $1 + 9 + 8 + 1 + 9 + 9 = 37$.

If the hundreds digit is 2, the numbers that maximize the sum must be 248 and 249, which give the result $2 + 4 + 8 + 2 + 4 + 9 = 29$; that is smaller than 37.

So the number on the left page is **198.**

15. One Hundred, Nine Tens, Six Ones

The number of objects in the hundreds column must be 0 or 1.

Let's first assume that it is 1. We then have to represent $196 - 100 = 96$ with 69 objects in the tens and the units columns.

Let's start with 0 in the tens and 69 in the units. This is too small ($0 + 69 = 69$, not 96), so we'll have to move some objects into the tens column. Every time we move one object from the units, we have subtracted 1 from the value, but since we have moved it to the tens, we have added 10 to the value. The net result is that we have added 9 to the value. Since our starting value is too small by 27 ($96 - 69 = 27$), we have to add 9 three times ($27/9 = 3$), so we have to put 3 items in the tens, leaving 66 in the units. Check: $10 \times 3 + 66 = 96$.

Let's now assume that the hundreds digit is 0. We then have to represent 196 with 70 objects in the tens and the units columns.

This time we start with $0 + 70 = 70$. Now our starting value is too small by 126 ($196 - 70 = 126$), so we have to add 9 fourteen times ($126/9 = 14$). We put 14 items in the tens, leaving 56 in the units. Check: $10 \times 14 + 56 = 196$.

Matthew's and Matilda's solutions are **(1, 3, 66)** and **(0, 14, 56).**

16. Six in a Rectangle

The 2 cannot go in *a,* in *c,* or in *e* since these are related to 1 (see Figure 1). So 2 can be in *b* or in *d.*

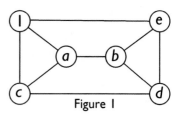
Figure 1

If 2 is in *b,* then 3 is in *a,* 4 in *e,* 5 in *a,* and 6 in *d.* This gives **the first solution,** shown in Figure 2.

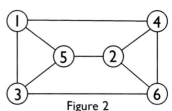
Figure 2

If 2 is in *d,* then 3 is in *c,* 4 in *e,* 5 in *c,* and 6 in *b.* This gives **the second solution,** shown in Figure 3.

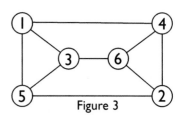
Figure 3

Notice that these two solutions correspond to each other if you exchange *a* with *c* and *b* with *d.*

17. The Bottle

When the bottle was half empty, it weighed 1,225 − 784 = 441 g less than when it was full. This difference represents the weight of half the juice in the bottle since it was half empty.

When the bottle was empty, another 441 g (half the juice weight) had disappeared and there remained only the weight of the bottle, that is, 784 − 441 = 343 g.

So the empty bottle weighed **343 g.**

18. Lolly's Lollipop

Mme. Bonbon has at least 50 centimes, in some combination of 5-centime, 10-centime, and 20-centime coins. She can give 5 centimes change (20 − 15), but she cannot give 35 centimes (50 − 15) or 85 centimes (100 − 15) change.

Because she can give 5 centimes, she must have at least one 5-centime coin. She cannot have any 10-centime coins, or with the 5-centime coin she would be able to give 15 centimes. Likewise, she must have no more than two 5-centime coins. These two facts together also ensure that she cannot give 35 centimes change.

Since she has at most 10 centimes in non-20-centime coins, in order to have at least 50 centimes she must have at least two 20-centime coins. But she cannot have four (or more) 20-centime coins, or with the 5-centime coin she would be able to give 85 centimes change.

So the possibilities are one or two 5-centime coins and two or three 20-centime coins. The combinations of these that add up to at least 50 centimes are 20 + 20 + 5 + 5, 20 + 20 + 20 + 5, and 20 + 20 + 20 + 5 + 5. Thus, Mme. Bonbon has **50, 65, or 70 centimes** in her cash register.

19. A Bag of Candy

When Matilda takes two candies, she has one more than Matthew since Matthew has taken one candy.

When Matilda takes four candies, she has two more than Matthew, the previous one and a new candy since Matthew has taken three candies instead of four.

When Matilda takes six candies, she has three more than Matthew, the previous ones and a new candy since Matthew has taken five candies instead of six.

So when Matilda has ten more candies than Matthew, she has taken candies from the bag ten times. Since there are no candies left in the bag, we can conclude that the bag had 1 + 2 + 3 + 4 + 5 + 6 + 7 + 8 + 9 + 10 + 11 + 12 + 13 + 14 + 15 + 16 + 17 + 18 + 19 + 20 candies.

This sum can be written in the following way:

$$
\begin{array}{rrrrrrrrrr}
1 & +\ 2 & +\ 3 & +\ 4 & +\ 5 & +\ 6 & +\ 7 & +\ 8 & +\ 9 & +10 \\
+20 & +19 & +18 & +17 & +16 & +15 & +14 & +13 & +12 & +11
\end{array}
$$

Clearly the two numbers in the same column always add up to 21. So the sum of the integers from 1 to 20 is equal to 10 × 21 = 210. The bag contained **210 candies.**

20. Skiing

Starting from the top, you work out the maximum total of points Bernard can get to reach any given square. To do this, working from the top to the bottom, the maximum at a square is the sum of its number and of the larger of the two cumulative totals immediately above it (or the only cumulative total immediately above it, if it is an edge square).

The greatest score Bernard can get is **48**, as shown by the gray squares.

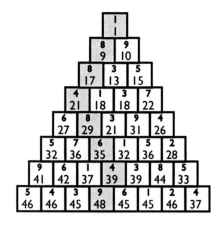

21. Enchanted Square

Let a, b, c, d, e, f, and g be the seven missing numbers. The equality between the two sums within the squares on the leftmost diagram below reads $1 + a + c + d = 7 + a + b + d$, which leads to $1 + c = b + 7$, or $c = b + 6$.

Following the other diagrams, you find the equalities:

$$1 + a = e + f$$
$$c + e = 7 + g$$
$$a + b = f + g$$

The equation $c = b + 6$ has only two possible solutions: $b = 2$ and $c = 8$, or $b = 3$ and $c = 9$.

Let's consider the first case. Then $c + e = 7 + g$ becomes $8 + e = 7 + g$, from which $g = e + 1$. Among all the possible solutions—$(e, g) = (3, 4)$, $(4, 5)$, or $(5, 6)$—the first and the third cases don't lead to a solution, and the second case leads to two distinct solutions (the middle two following).

50 Mathematical Puzzles and Problems ◆ Green Collection
©2001 Key Curriculum Press

Let's consider the second case. This time we find that $g = e + 2$. Among all the possible solutions—$(e, g) = (2, 4)$, $(4, 6)$, or $(6, 8)$, the first case leads to a single solution, the second one to two solutions, and the last case doesn't lead to any solution.

1	6	3
9	8	7
2	5	4

1	8	3
9	2	7
4	5	6

1	5	3
9	8	7
4	2	6

1	a	3
9	d	7
6	f	8

There are **five solutions**, shown below.

1	9	2
8	3	7
4	6	5

1	6	2
8	9	7
4	3	5

1	6	3
9	8	7
2	5	4

1	5	3
9	8	7
4	2	6

1	8	3
9	2	7
4	5	6

22. Melancholy

The magic square you have to fill in contains the same numbers as Dürer's. So its magic sum will be the same, namely, 34.

16	a	1	13
9	b	c	d
e	f	g	7
h	15	14	i

So a is equal to $34 - (16 + 1 + 13) = 34 - 30 = 4$.

On the fourth row, you already have a total of 29, so $h + i = 5$. Since 1 is already put in, $h + i = 2 + 3$ or $3 + 2$. If $h = 2$, e must be 7, but 7 is already put in. So $h = 3$, $i = 2$, $e = 6$, and $d = 12$.

Four numbers remain to be put in: 5, 8, 10, and 11. Since $b + c = 13$ and $c + g = 19$, it follows that $c = 8$, $b = 5$, $g = 11$, and f must be 10. See the **solution** at right.

16	4	1	13
9	5	8	12
6	10	11	7
3	15	14	2

It is amazing that all the magic properties of this square are still true, even though we considered only horizontal and vertical sums in constructing it.

23. The Incomplete Table

Label the table as shown at right. You find successively that

+	E	7	G	H
A	7	a	b	15
3	c	d	11	e
C	f	g	h	i
6	j	k	l	16

$d = 3 + 7 = 10$ $k = 6 + 7 = 13$ $H = 16 - 6 = 10$

$A = 15 - 10 = 5$ $a = 5 + 7 = 12$ $e = 3 + 10 = 13$

$E = 7 - 5 = 2$ $c = 3 + 2 = 5$ $G = 11 - 3 = 8$

$b = 5 + 8 = 13$ $j = 6 + 2 = 8$ $l = 6 + 8 = 14$

The third row remains to be filled in. The sum of the other three rows is

$(7 + 12 + 13 + 15) + (5 + 10 + 11 + 13) + (8 + 13 + 14 + 16) = 47 + 39 + 51 = 137$.

So the sum of the numbers in the third row is **63**.

Since these numbers are $C + 2$, $C + 7$, $C + 8$, and $C + 10$, you can easily work out that $4C = 63 - 27 = 36 = 4 \times 9$. So $C = 9$, enabling you to fill in the table.

The numbers written in the third row are **11, 16, 17, and 19.**

+	2	7	8	10
5	7	12	13	15
3	5	10	11	13
9	11	16	17	19
6	8	13	14	16

24. Lady Adelaide Adler

Consider two additions: the one written by Lady Adelaide and the usual addition.

a must equal 7, since in Lady Adelaide's method the left-hand "1" is the *units* digit of the answer. Then the two digits represented by dots must also add to 11 in *both* methods. These are the possibilities:

$$9 + 2 = 8 + 3 = 7 + 4 = 6 + 5 = 5 + 6 = 4 + 7 = 3 + 8 = 2 + 9 = 11$$

So there are 8 solutions: The number in the second row is **72, 73, 74, 75, 76, 77, 78,** or **79.**

```
   4 .              4 .
   a . +          +  a .
  -----           -----
   1 2 1           1 2 1

   Lady
 Adelaide's         Usual
  addition         addition
```

25. The Five Weights

The table shows how you can obtain all the weights from 1 lb to 24 lb, except 4 lb and 20 lb.

So you can obtain **22 different weights.**

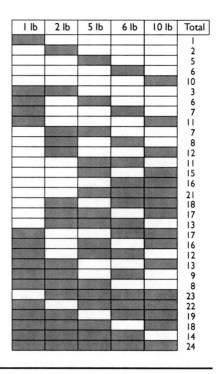

26. Mary's Flowers

On the first day, Mary cut as many flowers as her age.

On the second day, she cut as many flowers as twice her age.

On the third day, she cut as many flowers as 4 times her age.

On the fourth day, she cut as many flowers as 8 times her age.

On the fifth day, she cut as many flowers as 16 times her age, and this number is equal to her grandma's age, which is 60 years more than her own age.

So Mary's grandma's age is 16 times Mary's age, but it's also Mary's age plus 60 years. Let m = Mary's age. Then $16m = m + 60$. Solving this gives $15m = 60$, so Mary's age $m = 4$, and her grandma's age $m + 60 = 64$.

During these five days, Mary cut as many flowers as $1 + 2 + 4 + 8 + 16 = 31$ times her age, that is, $31 \times 4 = $ **124.**

27. The Eye of the Cyclops

Since we know that eight numbers are hidden by the mask, the hole in the mask cannot be on the edge of the multiplication table.

Trying a few examples, you quickly notice that the sum of the eight hidden numbers is equal to eight times the center number (you can prove it very simply by doing the calculation with two unknowns, x and y, so that "xy" reads as the central number). So the center number in our case is $288/8 = 36$.

x	2	3	4	5	6	7	8	9
2	4	6	8	10	12	14	16	18
3	6	9	12	15	18	21	24	27
4	8	12	16	20	24	28	32	36
5	10	15	20	25	30	35	40	45
6	12	18	24	30	36	42	48	54
7	14	21	28	35	42	49	56	63
8	16	24	32	40	48	56	64	72
9	18	27	36	45	54	63	72	81

You can verify that the eight surrounding numbers add up to 288:

$25 + 30 + 35 + 42 + 49 + 42 + 35 + 30 = 288$.

So the center number is **36.**

28. Marathon

The runners numbered 4, 5, and 6 were placed 1st, 2nd, and 3rd. So 5 (the only odd) got the only even: 2. Since 6 is divisible by 3, 6 must be in first place (since 1 is not divisible by 3) and 4 in third place.

Doing the same for the runners numbered 1, 2, and 3, you can see that runner 2 got the only odd place: 5. Since 3 is divisible by itself, 3 must be in fourth place and 1 finished last.

The runners' order on the finish line is **6, 5, 4, 3, 2, 1.**

29. Numerical Maze

In the figure, draw a bold line between two adjacent squares if they have no common divisor (except 1). Then you can see that there exist two different ways out: **95, 105, 28, 36, 117, 65, 26, 14, 18, 99, 45, 85, 34, 92, 46, 69, 96,** and, a possible variation: **119, 91, 133, 57, 111, 296, between 34 and 92.**

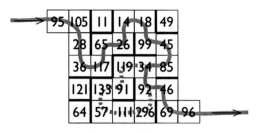

30. Granddad's Age

The birth years of Joss and Teresa are four-digit consecutive integers.

The sum of these digits cannot have the same parity, except in the case when a tens digit changes.

They were born after 1901 and before 1950 (since the sum of their ages in 2001 was more than 100). So five possibilities remain:

> 1909 and 1910 (the sums of the digits, respectively, are 19 and 11)
>
> **1919** and **1920** (the sums of the digits, respectively, are 20 and 12)
>
> 1929 and 1930 (the sums of the digits, respectively, are 21 and 13)
>
> 1939 and 1940 (the sums of the digits, respectively, are 22 and 14)
>
> 1949 and 1950 (the sums of the digits, respectively, are 23 and 15)

You can see that there is a single solution: Granddad Joss was born in **1919.**

31. The Smallest of the Great

First notice that every integer is a multiple of 1.

The smallest of Giles's numbers should be a multiple of 2, so it is even.

But it also has to be a multiple of 4 and 8. However, every multiple of 8 is a multiple of 4 and of 2, so it is sufficient to look for a multiple of 8.

This number should also be a multiple of 3 and of 9. However, every multiple of 9 is a multiple of 3, so it is sufficient to look for a multiple of 9.

Moreover, if a number is a multiple of 8 and 9, it is also a multiple of 72, so it is a multiple of 6, since $72 = 6 \times 12$.

This number should also be a multiple of 5 and of 10. Since it is a multiple of 8, it is a multiple of 2, so it is enough to say that it is a multiple of 5.

Finally, this number should be a multiple of 7, since that is not directly deduced from the previous remarks.

So we are looking for the smallest number that is a multiple of 8, 9, 5, and 7. It is the product of all these numbers: $8 \times 9 \times 5 \times 7 = 2,520$.

The smallest of Giles's numbers is **2,520.**

32. The Holey Alphabet

Let's find the number of letters having a hole, compared to those not having a hole, in each word:

quarter (3/7) finals (1/6) of (1/2) the (1/3) tenth (1/5) mathematical (4/12) and (2/3) logical (3/7) championship (3/12)

$$7 + 6 + 2 + 3 + 5 + 12 + 3 + 7 + 12 = 57$$
$$3 + 1 + 1 + 1 + 1 + 4 + 2 + 3 + 3 = 19$$

So the expression "quarter finals of the tenth mathematical and logical championship" has 57 letters, among which there are 19 holey letters and $57 - 19 = 38$ non-holey letters.

So, each time you print out this expression, you use the equivalent of $38 + 3 \times 19 = 95$ usual letters.

Since $1,000,000 = 95 \times 10,526 + 30$, the printer can print the expression 10,526 times, with the equivalent of 30 usual letters remaining.

$30 = (7 + 3 \times 2) + (6 + 1 \times 2) + (2 + 1 \times 2) + (3 + 1 \times 2)$, that is, "quarter finals of the." So the last printed letter will be an **e.**

---

33. The Mathematical Cook

Let's study what happens at the beginning:

A-B-C-D-E-**E**-A-B-C-D-**D**-E-A-B-C-**C**-D-E-A-B-**B**-C-D-E-A-**A** ...

We notice that after the 25th slice, the 26th slice is put on plate *A* like the first one, and that the 27th is put on plate *B* like the 2nd one, the 28th like the 3rd one, and so on; the moves repeat periodically every 25 slices.

Since 1,995 = 79 × 25 + 20, the slice numbered 1,995 will be put on the same plate as the 20th, that is, plate *B*.

So Julius puts the last slice on plate **B**.

A	B	C	D	E
1	2	3	4	5 **6**
7	8	9	10 **11**	12
13	14	15 **16**	17	18
19	20 **21**	22	23	24
25 **26**	...			
				...
1,975 **1,976**	1,977	1,978	1,979	1,980 **1,981**
1,982	1,983	1,984	1,985 **1,986**	1,987
1,988	1,989	1,990 **1,991**	1,992	1,993
1,994	**1,995**			

34. Spring Forward, Fall Back

If you represent the move from one letter to another, you obtain the diagram shown here.

So, calling A her first letter, Juliet moves along a circle with seven letters.

Dividing 96 by 7 gives a quotient of 13 and a remainder of 5. So Juliet will achieve 13 complete circles and then five more letters: A, E, I, M, and J.

Her 96th letter will be a **J** (as in **J**uliet).

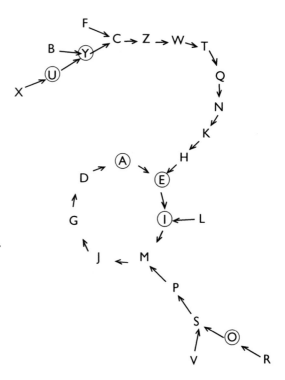

35. Zuzu's Petals

First method:

Let's first assume that Zuzu plucks the 95 petals of the mathflower without removing the new ones. Since $95 = 5 \times 19$ she says the sequence "a little, a lot, passionately, in love, not at all" 19 times, and 19 new petals have grown up.

Now, Zuzu plucks the 19 new petals without plucking the *new* new ones.

Since $19 = 5 \times 3 + 4$ she says the sequence "a little, a lot, passionately, in love, not at all" 3 times, and 3 new petals have grown up, added to the remaining 4 petals.

Since $7 = 5 \times 1 + 2$, she says the complete sequence once, 1 new petal grows, and 3 petals remain. When plucking these petals, she says "a little, a lot, passionately."

So Zuzu has plucked $95 + 19 + 3 + 1 = $ **118 petals,** and she says **"passionately"** while plucking the last one.

Second method:

Each time Zuzu plucks 5 petals, she says the complete sequence "a little, a lot, passionately, in love, not at all," and a new petal grows. So this operation corresponds in fact to reducing the total number of petals by 4 units and always beginning the sequence by "a little."

Since $95 = 4 \times 23 + 3$, Zuzu says the complete sequence 23 times and plucks $23 \times 5 = 115$ petals. Three more petals then remain.

So Zuzu plucks $115 + 3 = $ **118 petals,** and she says the third word of the sequence, which is **"passionately."**

36. Quotient = rosiviD

You have to try all the products shown in the figure. If the product is greater than 100,000 or the remainder is larger than one of the factors, it cannot be a correct answer.

$100,000 - 109 \times 901 = 1,791$, so the remainder is too large. $(1,791 > 901)$, and $129 \times 921 > 100,000$.

$100,000 - 108 \times 801 = 13,492$, which is too large a remainder.

1_9 × 9_1
1_8 × 8_1
1_7 × 7_1
1_6 × 6_1
1_5 × 5_1
2_4 × 4_2
2_3 × 3_2

$100,000 - 127 \times 721 = 8,433$, which is too large a remainder, and $137 \times 731 > 100,000$.

$100,000 - 146 \times 641 = 6,414$, which is too large a remainder, and $156 \times 651 > 100,000$.

$100,000 - 175 \times 571 = 75$ works, since $75 < 175 < 571$.

$100,000 - 214 \times 412 = 11,832$, which is too large a remainder, and $234 \times 432 > 100,000$.

$100,000 - 263 \times 362 = 4,794$, which is too large a remainder, and $273 \times 372 > 100,000$.

Finally, if the hundreds digit of the smallest of the two numbers is greater than or equal to 3, the product of this number and its reverse must be greater than 100,000.

So the problem has **two solutions:** The divisor can be either **175** or **571.**

37. Phone

First, notice that $3 \times 6 = 18$. If there had been six calls, since each call rings at least three times there would have been at least 18 rings. So the phone rang fewer than six times.

Next, notice that $4 \times 4 = 16$. If there had been four calls, since each call rings at most four times there would have been at most 16 rings. So the phone rang more than four times.

Only one solution remains: There have been **five calls**—three calls of three rings and two calls of four rings.

38. Lots of Minuses

We will show that after simplifying by eliminating parentheses we always obtain an expression of the form $1 - 2 \pm 3 \pm 4 \pm 5 \pm 6$; that is, we will show that except for 1, which must always be added, and 2, which must always be subtracted, the other numbers, depending on the location of the parentheses, can be either added or subtracted. Let's call the most "outside" parentheses "Level 1 parentheses." We will call the most "outside" parentheses within Level 1 parentheses "Level 2 parentheses," and so on. Each of the numbers 3, 4, 5, and 6 will be subtracted if it is outside of parentheses or immediately after an opening (that is, left) Level 1 or other odd-level parenthesis. It will be added if it is immediately after an opening Level 2 or other even-level parenthesis. Therefore, we can ignore parentheses and instead consider how many expressions of the form $1 - 2 \pm 3 \pm 4 \pm 5 \pm 6$ there are. Since each of the numbers 3 through 6 has two possibilities (added or subtracted), there are $2 \times 2 \times 2 \times 2 = 2^4 = 16$ possible sums.

Are all of these sums different?

Trying all the possibilities shows that two of them are the same, resulting from the equality $3 + 6 = 4 + 5$. So there are **15 different results.**

Note: The locations of parentheses shown below are not the only way to produce these sums. For example, $1 - (2 - 3) - (4 - 5) - 6 = 1 - (2 - (3 - (4 - (5 - 6)))) = 1 - 2 + 3 - 4 + 5 - 6$.

$$1 - 2 - 3 - 4 - 5 - 6 = -19$$
$$1 - 2 - 3 - 4 - (5 - 6) = 1 - 2 - 3 - 4 - 5 + 6 = -7$$
$$1 - 2 - 3 - (4 - 5) - 6 = 1 - 2 - 3 - 4 + 5 - 6 = -9$$
$$1 - 2 - (3 - 4) - 5 - 6 = 1 - 2 - 3 + 4 - 5 - 6 = -11$$
$$1 - (2 - 3) - 4 - 5 - 6 = 1 - 2 + 3 - 4 - 5 - 6 = -13$$
$$1 - 2 - 3 - (4 - 5 - 6) = 1 - 2 - 3 - 4 + 5 + 6 = 3$$
$$1 - 2 - (3 - 4) - (5 - 6) = 1 - 2 - 3 + 4 - 5 + 6 = 1$$
$$1 - (2 - 3) - 4 - (5 - 6) = 1 - 2 + 3 - 4 - 5 + 6 = -1$$
$$1 - 2 - (3 - 4 - 5) - 6 = 1 - 2 - 3 + 4 + 5 - 6 = -1$$
$$1 - (2 - 3) - (4 - 5) - 6 = 1 - 2 + 3 - 4 + 5 - 6 = -3$$
$$1 - (2 - 3 - 4) - 5 - 6 = 1 - 2 + 3 + 4 - 5 - 6 = -5$$
$$1 - 2 - (3 - 4 - 5 - 6) = 1 - 2 - 3 + 4 + 5 + 6 = 11$$
$$1 - (2 - 3) - (4 - 5 - 6) = 1 - 2 + 3 - 4 + 5 + 6 = 9$$
$$1 - (2 - 3 - 4) - (5 - 6) = 1 - 2 + 3 + 4 - 5 + 6 = 7$$
$$1 - (2 - 3 - 4 - 5) - 6 = 1 - 2 + 3 + 4 + 5 - 6 = 5$$
$$1 - (2 - 3 - 4 - 5 - 6) = 1 - 2 + 3 + 4 + 5 + 6 = 17$$

39. Jacob's Ladder

The diagram shows that the greatest possible length of the double ladder staying within the limits of the security rules (that is, to put the hooks on the rung immediately below CD) is

$11 \times 20 + 11 \times 20 - 4 \times 20$

$= (11 + 11 - 4) \times 20$

$= 18 \times 20$

$= 360$ cm

$= \textbf{3.60 m}$

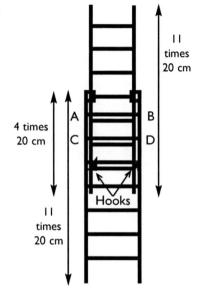

40. The Eraser

Two numbers adding up to 12 are 5 and 7, and 4 and 8. Since $8 - 4 = 4$ and $7 - 5 = 2$, remove 7 and 5.

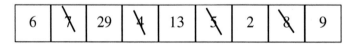

The other two numbers adding up to 12 are 4 and 8, and they have a product of 32. So remove 8 and 4.

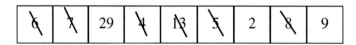

Two numbers whose difference is 7 are 9 and 2, and 13 and 6. Since $13 \times 6 = 78$, remove 13 and 6.

| 6 | 7 | 29 | 4 | 13 | 5 | 2 | 8 | 9 |

Three numbers remain: 29, 9, and 2. We need to find which two numbers, when dividing one by the other, give a quotient of 3 and a remainder of 2.

So remove 29 and 9.

The remaining number is **2.**

41. Menhir's Obelisks

So all the areas of the small obelisk are 1/16 (1/4 × 1/4) those of the large obelisk, and the volume is 1/64 (1/4 × 1/4 × 1/4), giving 8 metric tons/64 = 0.125 metric ton = **125 kg.**

42. Of Mice and Sacks

Let's look at the movie of this gluttonous adventure!

In the diagram, the nights are in bold.

The total number of sacks of wheat eaten is then 10 + 8 + 6 + 4 + 2 = **30.**

	Yesterday	Today	Tomorrow	The day after tomorrow	After 3 days	After 4 days
Number of mice alive	40	32	24	16	8	0
Number of sacks eaten		**10**	**8**	**6**	**4**	**2**	

43. The Umbrellas of Colorbourg

The difference d between the green and the yellow umbrellas is equal to the difference between the yellow and the red umbrellas, so if we transformed d green umbrellas into d red umbrellas, there would be the same number of umbrellas in each color. Since we would not have changed the number of yellow umbrellas, there are 69/3 = 23 yellow umbrellas.

Since there are 15 red umbrellas, $d = 23 - 15 = 8$ and $23 + 8 = $ **31 green umbrellas.**

44. The Two-Key Pocket Calculator

Let's begin the problem from the end: Start with 100 and then try to see which numbers lead to 100 in one push, then which numbers lead to the previous ones in one push, and so on.

On the diagram, each number that cannot be obtained from the two operations allowed is marked with an ×.

Looking at this diagram, you can see that at least **five keys** must be pressed on the calculator: $(1 \times 5 + 5 + 5 + 5) \times 5 = 100$.

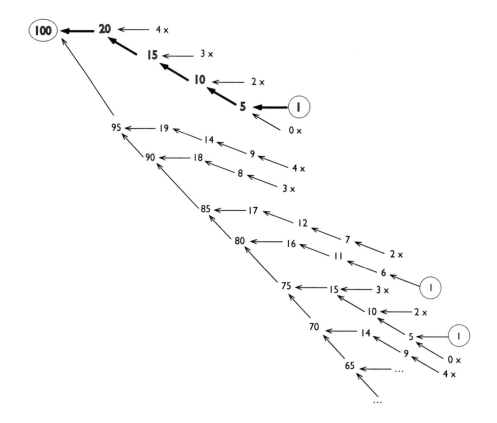

45. Thomas's Threes

All Thomas's numbers will be multiples of 3. The table shows how to get the first multiples of 3.

Studied number	Expression using the smallest possible number of 3's	Number of 3's used	Studied number	Expression using the smallest possible number of 3's	Number of 3's used
3	3	1	30	$3 \times 3 \times 3 + 3$	4
6	$3 + 3$	2	33	$3 \times 3 \times 3 + 3 + 3$	5
9	3×3	2	36	$3(3 \times 3 + 3)$	4
12	$3 \times 3 + 3$	3	39	$3(3 \times 3 + 3) + 3$	5
15	$3 \times 3 + 3 + 3$	4	42	$3(3 \times 3 + 3) + 3 + 3$	6
18	$3(3 + 3)$	3	45	$3(3 \times 3 + 3 + 3)$	5
21	$3(3 + 3) + 3$	4	48	$3(3 \times 3 + 3 + 3) + 3$	6
24	$3(3 + 3) + 3 + 3$	5	51	$3(3 \times 3 + 3 + 3) + 3 + 3$	7
27	$3 \times 3 \times 3$	3	54	$3(3 \times 3 + 3 \times 3)$	5

Clearly, the best solution is to use multiplication when possible, that is, when the number is a multiple of 9 (except 3). The rule is simple: If the number is a multiple of 9, first divide it by 3 and try to write the quotient with 3's. If not, as with 96, decompose it as a sum of two multiples of 3.

In the table at right, the minimum number of 3's needed to write a given number is shown in parentheses.

$96 = 3 + 93$	$(1 + \ldots)$
$96 = 6 + 90$	$(2 + \ldots)$
$96 = 9 + 87$	$(2 + \ldots)$
$96 = 12 + 84$	$(3 + \ldots)$
$96 = 15 + 81$	$(4 + \ldots)$
$96 = 18 + 78$	$(4 + \ldots)$
$96 = 21 + 75$	$(5 + \ldots)$
$96 = 24 + 72$	$(6 + \ldots)$
$96 = 27 + 69$	$(3 + \ldots)$
$96 = 30 + 66$	$(4 + \ldots)$
$96 = 33 + 63$	$(5 + \ldots)$
$96 = 36 + 60$	$(4 + \ldots)$
$96 = 42 + 57$	$(5 + \ldots)$
$96 = 45 + 54$	$(5 + \ldots)$
$96 = 48 + 51$	$(6 + \ldots)$

Let's try the decompositions containing a multiple of 9.
$96 = 6 + 3 \times 30$: The first table shows that we need the digit 3 four times to obtain 30. So we need $2 + 1 + 4 = 7$ digits to write 96.

$96 = 15 + 3 \times 27$: The first table shows that we need the digit 3 three times to write 27. So we need $4 + 1 + 3 = 8$ digits to write 96.

$96 = 24 + 3 \times 24$: The first table shows that we need the digit 3 six times to write 24. So we need $6 + 1 + 6 = 13$ digits to write 96.

$96 = 33 + 3 \times 21$: The first table shows that we need the digit 3 five times to write 21. So we need $5 + 1 + 5 = 11$ digits to write 96.

$96 = 45 + 3 \times 18$: The first table shows that we need the digit 3 four times to write 18. So we need $5 + 1 + 4 = 10$ digits to write 96.

So we need at least 7 digits to write 96, and there exists a single minimum solution: **$3 + 3 + 3(3 \times 3 \times 3 + 3)$. This expression uses the digit 3 seven times.**

46. The Maze

The diagram shows my moves in the maze, producing the message:

M A T H L O G G A M E S M

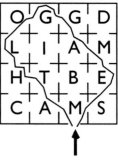

47. Zigzag

The diagram shows that I get back to A in **17 steps.**

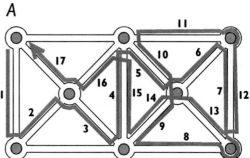

48. Marion's String

Here is one of the many possible routes:

50 Mathematical Puzzles and Problems ♦ *Green Collection*
©2001 Key Curriculum Press

49. The Shortest Word

A B A B A B A A B A A B.

Let's replace the first two letters: A B with B A A: B A A A B A B A A B A A B.

You can then erase the three A's: B B A B A A B A A B and then the two B's: A B A A B A A B.

You then replace the first two letters A B once more with B A A: B A A A B A A B.

You can erase the three A's and then replace the second and third letters A B with B A A. There remains: B B A A A A B.

You erase the two B's and the three A's. Two letters remain: A B.

Even when replacing this word with B A A, you cannot apply a new simplifying rule.

It only remains to prove that there is no other way that would bring us to an even shorter word. Since there are five B's in the initial word and since you always remove two B's together, at least one B remains in the final word. Moreover, since we remove only 4 B's, it is impossible to get rid of all the A's.

So the shortest word little Ababa can get is **the two-letter word AB.**

50. The Mathematician's Snare

Sarah's sentence is true since Paris has three consonants (P, R, and S) and two vowels (A and I).

Naomi's sentence may be true or false. If it is true, Rachel's sentence is false, and if it is false, Rachel's sentence is true. So, between Naomi's and Rachel's sentences, one is true and one is false*.

You can then check that Alice's sentence is true (it is the sum of the first nine prime numbers**).

So there are at least three true sentences. Since Elizabeth's sentence is therefore false, there are exactly **three true sentences.**

---

*In fact, Naomi is right, but it has no influence on the solution, as we saw before.

**A prime number is a number that has only two positive integral divisors: 1 and itself.

51. Dominick's Dominoes

First notice that there is only one possible position for the double 9 and for the double 1. Then, the 4-1 being set, you can draw a line between all the other 1's and 4's. Then the remaining 1 in the lower right corner can go only with the 8. So the 1 and the 8 just below the 4-1 have to be separated. So this 1 goes with the 5, and the 8 goes with the 4. Thus, the 1 in the first column must go with the 9.

In the rightmost column, the 9 must go with the 5, so the double 8 is in the upper right corner. You can then deduce that the 9-8 is below this one, then that the 5-8 is on the top row. On the bottom, we must have the 4-9, which then forces the double 4, which finally forces the 4-5 and the double 5. Here is the **solution:**

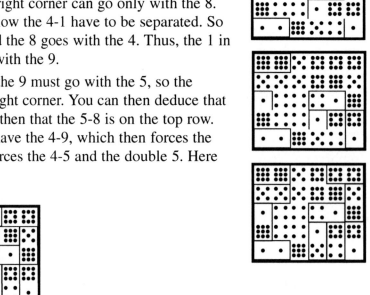

52. Awale

By playing a few rounds, we discover that the 11th move produces the same situation as the 4th, so that the 12th produces the same situation as the 5th, and so on. The game repeats with period 7, starting from the 4th position.

Since $1{,}995 = 7 \times 284 + 7$, the position after the 1,995th move is the same as the position after the 7th move, that is:

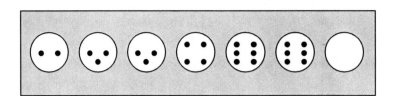